Symphony No. 4
in F Minor, Op. 36

Symphony No. 4
in F Minor, Op. 36

Peter Ilyitch
TCHAIKOVSKY

DOVER PUBLICATIONS, INC.
Mineola, New York

Published in Canada by General Publishing Company, Ltd., 30 Lesmill Road, Don Mills, Toronto, Ontario.

Published in the United Kingdom by Constable and Company, Ltd., 3 The Lanchesters, 162–164 Fulham Palace Road, London W6 9ER.

Bibliographical Note

This Dover edition, first published in 1998, is a republication of the work originally published by Breitkopf & Härtel, Leipzig, n.d.

International Standard Book Number: 0-486-40421-8

Manufactured in the United States of America
Dover Publications, Inc., 31 East 2nd Street, Mineola, N.Y. 11501

CONTENTS

To my best friend

Symphony No. 4
in F Minor, Op. 36
(1877–8)

INSTRUMENTATION

Piccolo [Kleine Flöte, Kl. Fl.]

2 Flutes [Flöten, Fl.]

2 Oboes [Oboen, Ob.]

2 Clarinets in A, B♭ ("B") [Klarinetten, Klar.]

2 Bassoons [Fagotte, Fag.]

4 Horns in F [Hörner, Hr.]

2 Trumpets in F [Trompeten, Trp.]

3 Trombones *(Alto, Tenor, Bass)*
  [Posaunen, Pos. *(Alt, Tenor, Baß / A., T., B.)*]
Tuba [Baßtuba, Btb.]

Timpani* [Pauken, Pk.]

Percussion
  Triangle [Triang(el)]
  Cymbals & Bass Drum
    [Beck(en) u(nd) Gr(osse) Tr(ommel)]

Violins 1, 2 [Violine, Viol.]

Violas [Viola]

Cellos [Violoncell, Vcll.]

Basses [Kontrabaß, Kb.]

*Timpani tunings include the following German terms:

As = A-flat	*Des* = D-flat
B = B-flat	*Fis* = F-sharp
	H = B-natural

Symphony No. 4
in F Minor, Op. 36

I

Andante sostenuto
1.
Flöten
2.
Oboen 1.2
Klarinetten 1.2 in B
Fagotte 1.2
1.2. in F
Hörner
3.4. in F
Trompeten 1.2 in F
Alt, Tenor
Posaunen
Baß
Baßtuba
Pauken in F, C, A
Andante sostenuto
Violine 1
Violine 2
Viola
Violoncello
Kontrabaß
Andante sostenuto

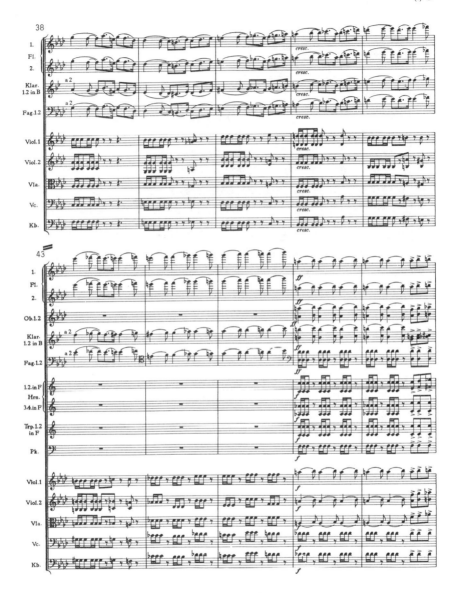

87

96

100
E
1.
Fl.
2.
Ob.1.2
Klar.
1.2 in B
mf dolce grazioso
a 2
Fag.1.2
mf dolce
1.2.in F
Hrn.
3.4.in F
Trp.1.2
in F
A.T.
Pos.
B.
Btb.
muta C in H, A in Fis
Pk.
E
Viol.1
p
Viol.2
p
Vla.
p
Vc.
p
Kb.
E p

105

110

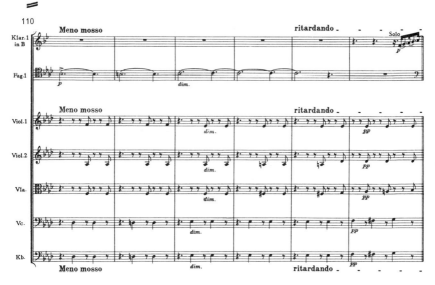

162

167
I
1.
Fl.
2.
Ob.1.2
Klar.
1.2 in B
Fag.1.2
1.2.in F
Hrn.
3.4.in F
a 2
Trp.1.2
in F
A.T.
Pos.
B.
Btb.
Pk.
Viol.1
Viol.2
Vla.
Vc.
Kb.
pizz.
arco
fff

172
1. Fl. 2.
Ob.1.2
Klar. 1.2 in B
Fag.1.2
1.2.inF Hrn. 3.4.inF
a 2
Trp.1.2 in F
A.T. Pos. B.
Btb.
Pk.
Viol.1
Viol.2
Vla.
Vc.
Kb.
fff

177

182
1.
Fl.
2.
Ob.1.2
Klar.
1.2 in B
Fag.1.2
a 2
1.2.in F
Hrn.
3.4.in F
Trp.1.2
in F
A.T.
Pos.
B.
Btb.
Pk.
Viol.1
Viol.2
Vla.
Vc.
Kb.

187

255

260
1.
Fl.
2.
Ob.1.2
Klar. 1.2 in B
a 2
Fag.1.2
1.2.in F
Hrn.
3.4.in F
Trp.1.2 in F
A. T.
Pos.
B.
Btb.
Pk.
Viol.1
Viol.2
Vla.
Vc.
Kb.

265

274

278

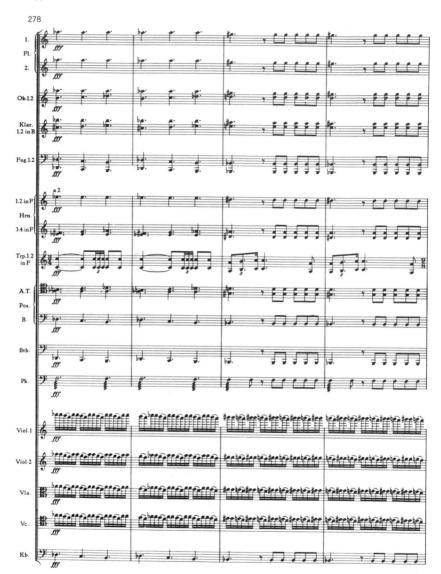

286

335

340

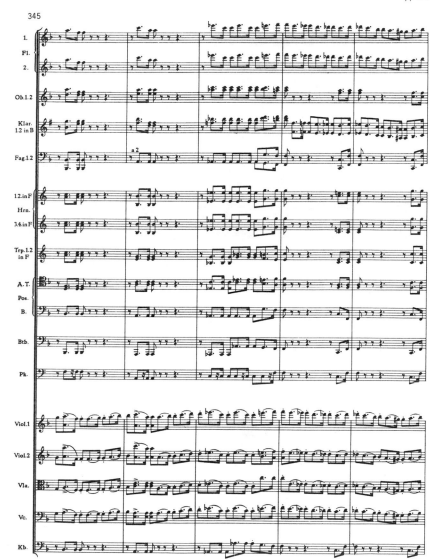

350

388

414

II

173

III. SCHERZO

Pizzicato ostinato

329
Viol.1
Viol.2
Vla.
Vc.
Kb.
dim.
p
339
H
pp
dim.
349
Kl.Fl.
1.
Fl.
2.
Ob.1.2
Klar.
1.2 in A
Fag.1
più f

359
Kl.Fl.
1.
Fl.
2.
Ob.1.2
Klar.
1.2 in A
Fag.1.2
1.2 in F
Hrn.
3.4 in F
Viol.1
Viol.2
Vla.
Vc.
Kb.
mf
f
a2
I
più f
369

378
Kl. Fl.
1.
Fl.
2.
Ob. 1.2
Klar. 1.2 in A
Fag. 1.2
1.2 in F
Hrn
3.4 in F
Viol. 1
Viol. 2
Vla.
Vc.
Kb.
a 2
cresc.
ff
388
Kl. Fl.
1.
Fl.
2.
Ob. 1.2
Klar. 1.2 in A
Fag. 1.2
1.2 in F
Hrn.
3.4 in F
Viol. 1
Viol. 2
Vla.
Vc.
Kb.
a 2

396
Kl.Fl.
1. Fl. 2.
Ob.1.2
Klar. 1.2 in A
Fag.1.2
1.2 in F Hrn. 3.4 in F
Trp.1.2 in F
A. T. Pos. B.
Pk.
Viol.1
Viol.2
Vla.
Vc.
Kb.
405
Hrn.2 in F
Trp.1 in F
A. T. Pos. B.
Viol.1
Viol.2
Vla.
Vc.
Kb.

IV. Finale

95

36
Kl. Fl.
1. Fl. 2.
Ob. 1.2
a 2
Klar. 1.2 in B
a 2
Fag. 1.2
1.2. in F
Hrn.
3.4. in F
Trp. 1.2 in F
A. T.
Pos.
B.
Btb.
Pk.
Beck. u. Gr. Tr.
Viol. 1
Viol. 2
Vla.
Vc.
Kb.
ff

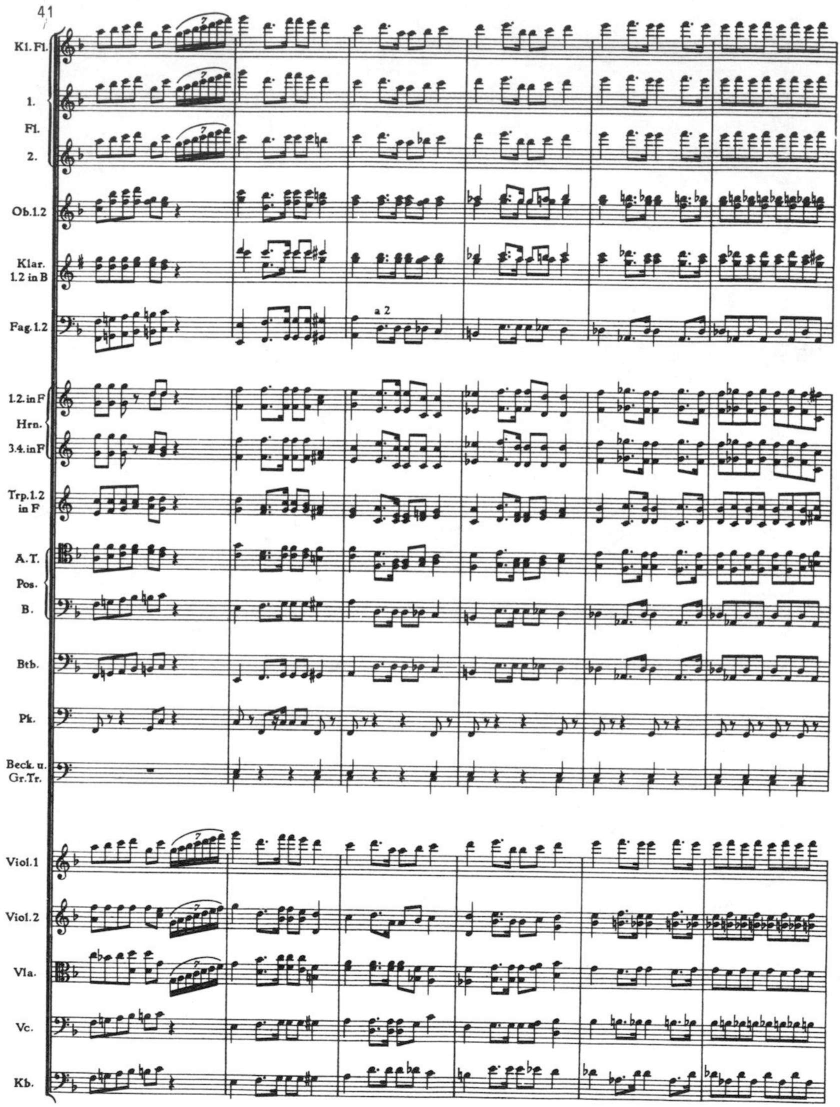
41
Kl. Fl.
1.
Fl.
2.
Ob. 1.2
Klar.
1.2 in B
Fag. 1.2
a 2
1.2. in F
Hrn.
3.4. in F
Trp. 1.2
in F
A. T.
Pos.
B.
Btb.
Pk.
Beck. u.
Gr. Tr.
Viol. 1
Viol. 2
Vla.
Vc.
Kb.

47
Kl. Fl.
1.
Fl.
2.
Ob.1.2
Klar.
1.2 in B
a 2
Fag.1.2
1.2. in F
Hrn.
3.4. in F
Trp.1.2
in F
A. T.
Pos.
B.
Btb.
Pk.
Gr.Tr.
8
Viol.1
Viol.2
Vla.
Vc.
Kb.

53
Kl. Fl.
1.
Fl.
2.
Ob. 1.2
Klar. 1.2 in B
Fag. 1.2
1.2. in F
Hrn.
3.4. in F
Trp. 1.2 in F
A. T.
Pos.
B.
Btb.
Pk.
Beck. u. Gr. Tr.
Viol. 1
Viol. 2
Vla.
Vc.
Kb.
fff
ff
8

107

111
Kl. Fl.
1.
Fl.
2.
Ob. 1.2
Klar. 1.2 in B
Fag. 1.2
1.2. in F
Hrn.
3.4. in F
Trp. 1.2 in F
A.T.
Pos.
B.
Btb.
Viol. 1
Viol. 2
Vla.
Vc.
Kb.
a 2
115

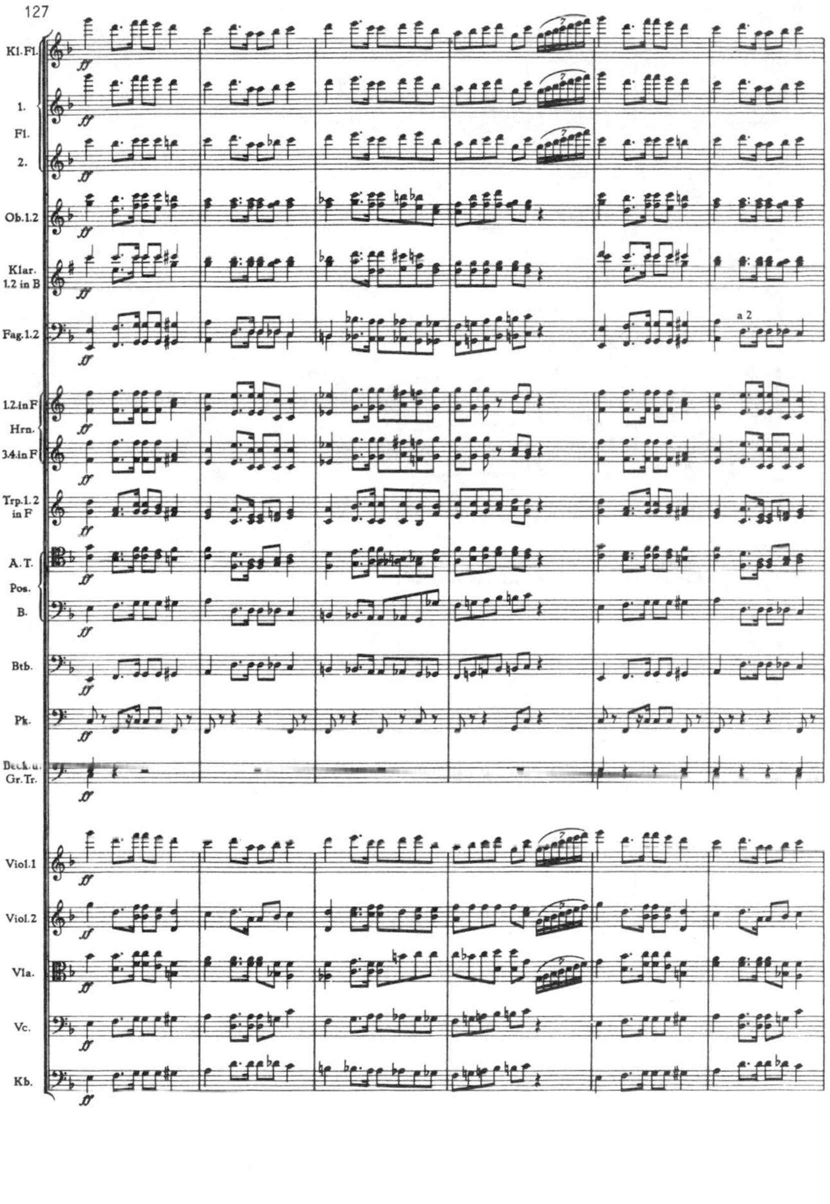
127
Kl. Fl.
1.
Fl.
2.
Ob. 1.2
Klar. 1.2 in B
Fag. 1.2
a 2
1.2. in F
Hrn.
3.4. in F
Trp. 1.2 in F
A. T.
Pos.
B.
Btb.
Pk.
Beck. u. Gr. Tr.
Viol. 1
Viol. 2
Vla.
Vc.
Kb.

133
Kl. Fl.
1.
Fl.
2.
Ob. 1.2
Klar. 1.2 in B
a 2
Fag. 1.2
1.2. in F
Hrn.
3.4. in F
Trp. 1.2 in F
A. T.
Pos.
B.
Btb.
Pk.
Beck. u. Gr. Tr.
8
Viol. 1
Viol. 2
Vla.
Vc.
Kb.

139

144

186

190

194

234
G
Kl. Fl.
1.
Fl.
2.
Ob.1.2
Klar.
1.2 in B
Fag.1.2
1.2.in F
Hrn.
3.4.in F
Pk.
Viol.1
Viol.2
Vla.
Vc.
Kb.
mf crescendo
crescendo
a 2
240
ff

259

272
Kl. Fl.
1.
Fl.
2.
Ob. 1.2
Klar.
1.2 in B
Fag. 1.2
1.2. in F
Hrn.
3.4. in F
Trp. 1.2
in F
a 2
A.T.
Pos.
B.
Btb.
Pk.
Triang.
Beck. u.
Gr. Tr.
8
Viol. 1
Viol. 2
Vla.
Vc.
Kb.

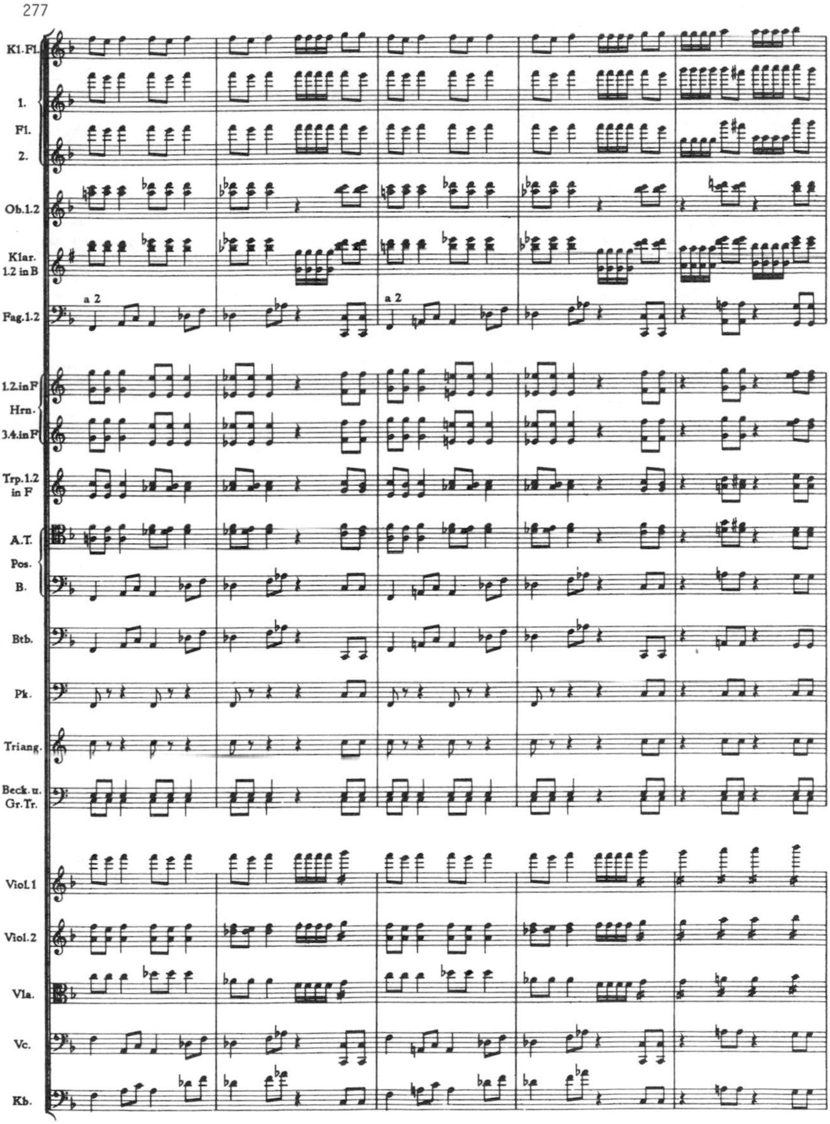
277
Kl. Fl.
1.
Fl.
2.
Ob. 1.2
Klar. 1.2 in B
a 2
Fag. 1.2
1.2. in F
Hrn.
3.4. in F
Trp. 1.2 in F
A.T.
Pos.
B.
Btb.
Pk.
Triang.
Beck. u. Gr. Tr.
Viol. 1
Viol. 2
Vla.
Vc.
Kb.

287

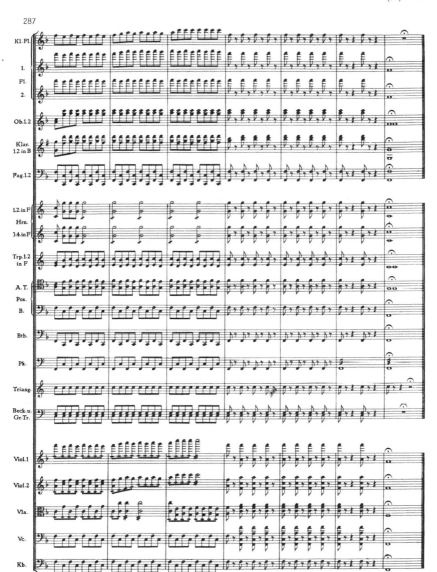

END OF EDITION

DOVER FULL-SIZE ORCHESTRAL SCORES

THE SIX BRANDENBURG CONCERTOS AND THE FOUR ORCHESTRAL SUITES IN FULL SCORE, Johann Sebastian Bach. Complete standard Bach-Gesellschaft editions in large, clear format. Study score. 273pp. 9 × 12. 23376-6 Pa. **$11.95**

COMPLETE CONCERTI FOR SOLO KEYBOARD AND ORCHESTRA IN FULL SCORE, Johann Sebastian Bach. Bach's seven complete concerti for solo keyboard and orchestra in full score from the authoritative Bach-Gesellschaft edition. 206pp. 9 × 12. 24929-8 Pa. **$11.95**

THE THREE VIOLIN CONCERTI IN FULL SCORE, Johann Sebastian Bach. Concerto in A Minor, BWV 1041; Concerto in E Major, BWV 1042; and Concerto for Two Violins in D Minor, BWV 1043. Bach-Gesellschaft edition. 64pp. 9⅜ × 12¼. 25124-1 Pa. **$6.95**

GREAT ORGAN CONCERTI, OPP. 4 & 7, IN FULL SCORE, George Frideric Handel. 12 organ concerti composed by great Baroque master are reproduced in full score from the *Deutsche Handelgesellschaft* edition. 138pp. 9⅜ × 12¼. 24462-8 Pa. **$8.95**

COMPLETE CONCERTI GROSSI IN FULL SCORE, George Frideric Handel. Monumental Opus 6 Concerti Grossi, Opus 3 and "Alexander's Feast" Concerti Grossi—19 in all—reproduced from most authoritative edition. 258pp. 9⅜ × 12¼. 24187-4 Pa. **$13.95**

LATER SYMPHONIES, Wolfgang A. Mozart. Full orchestral scores to last symphonies (Nos. 35–41) reproduced from definitive Breitkopf & Härtel Complete Works edition. Study score. 285pp. 9 × 12. 23052-X Pa. **$12.95**

PIANO CONCERTOS NOS. 17–22, Wolfgang Amadeus Mozart. Six complete piano concertos in full score, with Mozart's own cadenzas for Nos. 17–19. Breitkopf & Härtel edition. Study score. 370pp. 9⅜ × 12¼. 23599-8 Pa. **$16.95**

PIANO CONCERTOS NOS. 23–27, Wolfgang Amadeus Mozart. Mozart's last five piano concertos in full score, plus cadenzas for Nos. 23 and 27, and the Concert Rondo in D Major, K.382. Breitkopf & Härtel edition. Study score. 310pp. 9⅜ × 12¼. 23600-5 Pa. **$13.95**

COMPLETE CONCERTI GROSSI IN FULL SCORE, Arcangelo Corelli. All 12 concerti in the famous late nineteenth-century edition prepared by violinist Joseph Joachim and musicologist Friedrich Chrysander. 240pp. 8⅜ × 11¼. 25606-5 Pa. **$12.95**

PIANO CONCERTOS NOS. 11–16 IN FULL SCORE, Wolfgang Amadeus Mozart. Authoritative Breitkopf & Härtel edition of six staples of the concerto repertoire, including Mozart's cadenzas for Nos. 12–16. 256pp. 9⅜ × 12¼. 25468-2 Pa. **$12.95**

NUTCRACKER SUITE IN FULL SCORE, Peter Ilyitch Tchaikovsky. Among the most popular ballet pieces ever created—a complete, inexpensive, high-quality score to study and enjoy. 128pp. 9 × 12. 25379-1 Pa. **$8.95**

TONE POEMS, SERIES I: DON JUAN, TOD UND VERKLARUNG, and DON QUIXOTE, Richard Strauss. Three of the most often performed and recorded works in entire orchestral repertoire, reproduced in full score from original editions. Study score. 286pp. 9⅜ × 12¼. (Available in U.S. only) 23754-0 Pa. **$13.95**

TONE POEMS, SERIES II: TILL EULENSPIEGELS LUSTIGE STREICHE, ALSO SPRACH ZARATHUSTRA, and EIN HELDENLEBEN, Richard Strauss. Three important orchestral works, including very popular *Till Eulenspiegel's Merry Pranks,* reproduced in full score from original editions. Study score. 315pp. 9⅜ × 12¼. (Available in U.S. only) 23755-9 Pa. **$14.95**

DAS LIED VON DER ERDE IN FULL SCORE, Gustav Mahler. Mahler's masterpiece, a fusion of song and symphony, reprinted from the original 1912 Universal Edition. English translations of song texts. 160pp. 9 × 12. 25657-X Pa. **$9.95**

SYMPHONIES NOS. 1 AND 2 IN FULL SCORE, Gustav Mahler. Unabridged, authoritative Austrian editions of Symphony No. 1 in D Major ("Titan") and Symphony No. 2 in C Minor ("Resurrection"). 384pp. 8⅛ × 11. 25473-9 Pa. **$14.95**

SYMPHONIES NOS. 3 AND 4 IN FULL SCORE, Gustav Mahler. Two brilliantly contrasting masterworks—one scored for a massive ensemble, the other for small orchestra and soloist—reprinted from authoritative Viennese editions. 368pp. 9⅜ × 12¼. 26166-2 Pa. **$16.95**

SYMPHONY NO. 8 IN FULL SCORE, Gustav Mahler. Superb authoritative edition of massive, complex "Symphony of a Thousand." Scored for orchestra, eight solo voices, double chorus, boys' choir and organ. Reprint of Izdatel'stvo "Muzyka," Moscow, edition. Translation of texts. 272pp. 9⅜ × 12¼. 26022-4 Pa. **$12.95**

GREAT ROMANTIC VIOLIN CONCERTI IN FULL SCORE, Ludwig van Beethoven, Felix Mendelssohn and Peter Ilyitch Tchaikovsky. The Beethoven Op. 61, Mendelssohn, Op. 64 and Tchaikovsky, Op. 35 concertos reprinted from the Breitkopf & Härtel editions. 224pp. 9 × 12. 24989-1 Pa. **$10.95**

MAJOR ORCHESTRAL WORKS IN FULL SCORE, Felix Mendelssohn. Generally considered to be Mendelssohn's finest orchestral works, here in one volume are: the complete *Midsummer Night's Dream; Hebrides Overture; Calm Sea and Prosperous Voyage Overture;* Symphony No. 3 in A ("Scottish"); and Symphony No. 4 in A ("Italian"). Breitkopf & Härtel edition. Study score. 406pp. 9 × 12. 23184-4 Pa. **$18.95**

COMPLETE SYMPHONIES, Johannes Brahms. Full orchestral scores. No. 1 in C Minor, Op. 68; No. 2 in D Major, Op. 73; No. 3 in F Major, Op. 90; and No. 4 in E Minor, Op. 98. Reproduced from definitive Vienna Gesellschaft der Musikfreunde edition. Study score. 344pp. 9 × 12. 23053-8 Pa. **$14.95**

THE VIOLIN CONCERTI AND THE SINFONIA CONCERTANTE, K.364, IN FULL SCORE, Wolfgang Amadeus Mozart. All five violin concerti and famed double concerto reproduced from authoritative Breitkopf & Härtel Complete Works Edition. 208pp. 9⅜ × 12½. 25169-1 Pa. **$12.95**

17 DIVERTIMENTI FOR VARIOUS INSTRUMENTS, Wolfgang A. Mozart. Sparkling pieces of great vitality and brilliance from 1771–1779; consecutively numbered from 1 to 17. Reproduced from definitive Breitkopf & Härtel Complete Works edition. Study score. 241pp. 9⅜ × 12¼. 23862-8 Pa. **$13.95**

WATER MUSIC AND MUSIC FOR THE ROYAL FIREWORKS IN FULL SCORE, George Frideric Handel. Full scores of two of the most popular Baroque orchestral works performed today—reprinted from definitive Deutsche Handelgesellschaft edition. Total of 96pp. 8⅛ × 11. 25070-9 Pa. **$7.95**

FOURTH, FIFTH AND SIXTH SYMPHONIES IN FULL SCORE, Peter Ilyitch Tchaikovsky. Complete orchestral scores of Symphony No. 4 in F minor, Op. 36; Symphony No. 5 in E minor, Op. 64; Symphony No. 6 in B minor, "Pathetique," Op. 74. Study score. Breitkopf & Härtel editions. 480pp. 9⅜ × 12¼. 23861-X Pa. **$19.95**

ROMEO AND JULIET OVERTURE AND CAPRICCIO ITALIEN IN FULL SCORE, Peter Ilyitch Tchaikovsky. Two of Russian master's most popular compositions in high quality, inexpensive reproduction. From authoritative Russian edition. 208pp. 8⅜ × 11½. 25217-5 Pa. **$10.95**

DAPHNIS AND CHLOE IN FULL SCORE, Maurice Ravel. Definitive full-score edition of Ravel's rich musical setting of a Greek fable by Longus is reprinted here from the original French edition. 320pp. 9⅜ × 12¼. (Not available in France or Germany) 25826-2 Pa. **$15.95**

THREE GREAT ORCHESTRAL WORKS IN FULL SCORE, Claude Debussy. Three favorites by influential modernist: *Prélude à l'Après-midi d'un Faune, Nocturnes,* and *La Mer.* Reprinted from early French editions. 279pp. 9 × 12. 24441-5 Pa. **$13.95**

SYMPHONY IN D MINOR IN FULL SCORE, César Franck. Superb, authoritative edition of Franck's only symphony, an often-performed and recorded masterwork of late French romantic style. 160pp. 9 × 12. 25373-2 Pa. **$9.95**

THE GREAT WALTZES IN FULL SCORE, Johann Strauss, Jr. Complete scores of eight melodic masterpieces: The Beautiful Blue Danube, Emperor Waltz, Tales of the Vienna Woods, Wiener Blut, four more. Authoritative editions. 336pp. 8⅜ × 11¼. 26009-7 Pa. **$14.95**

THE FIREBIRD IN FULL SCORE (Original 1910 Version), Igor Stravinsky. Handsome, inexpensive edition of modern masterpiece, renowned for brilliant orchestration, glowing color. Authoritative Russian edition. 176pp. 9⅜ × 12¼. (Available in U.S. only) 25535-2 Pa. **$10.95**

PETRUSHKA IN FULL SCORE: Original Version, Igor Stravinsky. The definitive full-score edition of Stravinsky's masterful score for the great Ballets Russes 1911 production of *Petrushka.* 160pp. 9⅜ × 12¼. (Available in U.S. only) 25680-4 Pa. **$9.95**

MAJOR ORCHESTRAL WORKS IN FULL SCORE, Felix Mendelssohn. Generally considered to be Mendelssohn's finest orchestral works, here in one volume are: the complete *Midsummer Night's Dream; Hebrides Overture; Calm Sea and Prosperous Voyage Overture;* Symphony No. 3 in A ("Scottish"); and Symphony No. 4 in A ("Italian"). Breitkopf & Härtel edition. Study score. 406pp. 9 × 12. 23184-4 Pa. **$18.95**